1. Aberdeen
2. Aberdeenshire
3. Arran & Ayrshire
4. Argyll
5. Southern Argyll
6. The Borders
7. The Cairngorms
8. Caithness & Sutherland
9. Dumfries and Galloway
10. Dundee & Angus
11. Edinburgh
12. Fife, Kinross & Clackmannan
13. Glasgow
14. Inverness
15. The Isle of Skye
16. Lanarkshire
17. Lochaber
18. Loch Lomond, Cowal & Bute
19. The Lothians
20. Moray
21. Mull & Iona
22. Orkney
23. The Outer Hebrides
24. Perthshire
25. Ross & Cromarty
26. Royal Deeside
27. Shetland
28. Stirling & The Trossachs

The remaining three books, Caledonia, Distinguished Distilleries and Scotland's Mountains, feature locations throughout the country so are not included in the above list.

PICTURING SCOTLAND

MULL & IONA

NESS PUBLISHING

2   Mull is blessed with a number of exquisite beaches. The one seen here at Calgary in the north of the island is a first-rate example. See also p.21.

MULL & IONA

Welcome to Mull & Iona!

The islands of Mull and Iona exude majesty, mystery and an almost magical ability to mount an ever-changing presentation of mood and colour with each passing day. Given their location as islands on the edge of the Atlantic Ocean, their maritime climate delivers a different character with every shift in the weather.

This is no place to be in a hurry as to rush is to miss something – the fleeting glimpse of an otter, the fly-past of an eagle or the momentary feeling that one should simply pause for a moment – and just . . . watch.

With an area of 875.35 square kilometres (337.97 square miles), Mull is the fourth-largest Scottish island and also the fourth-largest island of Great Britain. But it might *feel* larger: a journey across Mull from the ferry port of Craignure in the east to Fionnphort in the west is likely to take up to an hour-and-a-half, but will cover fewer than 40 miles in the process – the joy of single-track roads! According to the 2011 census, the usual resident population of Mull was 2,800, about a quarter of whom lived in Tobermory, its colourful capital.

No tour of Mull can be made without mentioning its geological formation. A geological survey of Scotland in 1924 found that Mull featured the most complicated igneous centre ever examined in the world at that time. About 60 million years ago, a volcanic eruption near what we now know as Ben More on Mull began smothering this area with layer after layer of molten lava to a

Early on a Mull morning, the view north-east from Grasspoint sees the first ferry of the day from Oban to Craignure making its way through the skerries and islets that line its route. 5

height of an estimated 2,000m/6,000ft. Many millennia later, when the lava had cooled and the dust had settled, glaciers began carving out the glens and hillsides from the basalt mass. The intermittent layers of lava create Mull's distinctive terraced landscape. The sea level eventually dropped after the Ice Age, leaving raised beaches and the sea caves hanging up on hillsides well above the sea. Gradually, weather erosion filed off the sharp edges and soil accumulated. The basalt columns seen along the coast were formed when molten lava cooled and crystallised. This action is the same that formed the great columns on Staffa and the Giant's Causeway in Northern Ireland.

Celtic Christianity came to Scotland as a result of the missionary work of St Columba (521–597) and those who

6   As the ferry *Isle of Mull* approaches Craignure, anticipation grows.

followed him. He established a monastery on the Isle of Iona in 563. In the 12th century a Benedictine abbey and a nunnery were founded there, which remained the principal religious houses of the Isles until the Scottish Reformation from 1560. As the cradle of Christianity in Scotland and through the ongoing work of the Iona Community, Iona remains a major focus of Christian pilgrimage in Scotland, a sacred site which draws people from all over the world.

This book is set out as journey around Mull, taking a route that begins in the north-east of the island at its capital, Tobermory. From there it explores the northern parts, after which it travels through the western and central areas. From there we turn to the eastern extremity before working across Mull's southern districts, en route to the world-famous pilgrimage island of Iona, finishing off the tour with an excursion to the remarkable island of Staffa. In relation to the compact nature of the territory, it will be a journey of amazing variety and stunning scenery.

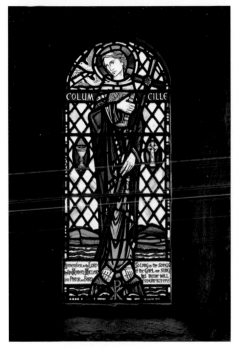

W. Wilson's stained-glass window of 1965 in Iona Abbey which commemorates the Revd Kenneth MacLeod.

8   Mull's 'capital' is the delightful port of Tobermory. The only town on the island, it has a population
of 700 and provides one of Scotland's, let alone Mull's, most iconic views thanks to the colourfully

painted buildings that line the waterfront. It is also known to many as 'Balamory', its fictional name in the well-known children's TV series.

10 Tobermory was built as a fishing port in the late 18th century because of its excellent south-east facing natural harbour, which can be appreciated in this view from the upper part of the town.

Tobermory derives its name from the Gaelic 'Tobar Mhoire' meaning the Well of Mary.
The village looks as attractive by night as it does by day.

12 Local businesses provide wildlife-watching excursions including boat trips to see dolphins, seals and seabirds. This is an evening view of Tobermory Bay, as always, full of boats.

Tobermory Distillery is Mull's only distillery, founded in 1798 by John Sinclair. It produces **13** *Tobermory* and *Ledaig* whiskies, both of which are available in several age expressions.

14 A few miles north-west of Tobermory, Glengorm Castle overlooks the Atlantic with views across to the islands of the Outer Hebrides, Rum and Canna. The Castle was built in 1860 and overlooks

ancient sites such as this group of standing stones. Beyond, at the headland, are the remains
of Dun Ara Castle, possibly a medieval hall-house.

16 Tracking inland from Tobermory involves cutting through hilly country from where this panorama of Loch Frisa and beyond is captured. The prominent peak on the right is Beinn Talaidh, 761m/2496ft.

This is the route that winds westwards towards the beautifully situated village of Dervaig. 17
The pencil-shaped structure towards the left is the church's unusual tower.

18 Just south of Dervaig is the Old Byre Heritage Centre, a 'must' for anyone who wants to absorb the
history of Mull. This is a model of an early monastic settlement.

The tiny settlement of Croig sits on an inlet on Mull's north coast from where this winter scene **19** includes the snow-capped mountains of the distant island of Rum.

20 Continuing westwards from Dervaig we reach Calgary, home of Calgary Art in Nature and this quirky 'take' on the idea of a boathouse, or houseboat – depending on how you look at it!

First seen back on pages 2-3, Calgary's wonderful beach has a distinctly tropical look to it on those **21** sunny, tranquil spring and summer days of which Mull has a goodly share.

22 Agriculture on Mull is mostly confined to suitable pockets of land scattered around the island. Here at Treshnish, looking towards Treshnish Point, some farm equipment takes a rest.

Mull also contains pockets of ancient native forest. The term 'rainforest' has a different meaning in **23** Scotland: these stunted and contorted oaks by Loch Tuath reflect harsh conditions.

24 Mull is a mountainous island, with a range of peaks running east to west across the heart of its landscape. Viewed from the summit point of the road from Calgary to Kilninian, Loch Tuath is in

the foreground with Ben More, Mull's highest peak, taking centre stage. Also in view to its left are A'Chioch and Beinn Fhada.

26 On the north side of Loch Tuath, Eas Fors is a waterfall of two halves. Left: the upper section cascades off the plateau and, right, the lower section drops straight down to the sea.

A couple of miles south of Eas Fors we come to Ulva Ferry where, amid photographically perfect **27** conditions, an array of small boats lie at anchor, making a picture-perfect scene.

28 The narrows here provide a convenient location for the foot passenger ferry that connects Mull to the Isle of Ulva. Ulva is the perfect location for a day of peaceful exploration, in which its

geological features can be closely examined. In this picture of the south side of Ulva, basalt columns **29** and heather-clad terraces grace this lava-layered landscape.

30 Left: Mull is one of the locations in Scotland where white-tailed sea eagles have been re-introduced. Specialist boat trips offer a close-up view! Right: ospreys have also re-established themselves here.

Located in Gruline, Macquarie's Mausoleum is the final resting place of Lachlan Macquarie, born on Ulva **31** in 1761 and later described as 'The Father of Australia' due to his Governorship of New South Wales.

32 From Gruline, it's just a few miles east to Salen and Aros on Mull's east coast.
Here on a calm day of low light, Aros Castle is among the features reflected in the bay.

Ben More, left of centre, is Mull's only Munro (Scottish mountains higher than 3,000ft/914m) and **33** stands 966m/3169ft high. The view from the east in Glen More shows off its most dramatic profile.

34 The most popular route up Ben More is from Dhisheig on Loch na Keal. As the ascent progresses, the north-westerly view takes in Loch na Keal, Ulva on the left and Loch Tuath beyond the narrows.

From Ben More's summit, to the east is A'Chioch (the peak on the right on p.33), connected to **35** Ben More by the challenging A'Chioch ridge. Warm rising air is constantly turning to cloud.

36 Ben More's propensity for creating cloud means it can often be murky at the top while it remains sunny below, as seen here looking north towards the head of Loch na Keal.

Left: west of Ben More, the lava terraces so typical of Mull are seen in sharp relief below Dunan nan **37** Nighean. Right: the base of the same crags rises above the road that winds along this stretch of coast.

38 The road soon turns south, opening up vistas that take in the islands west of Mull. The rainbow leans over Lunga – and it was from out there, on the sea, that the next picture was taken,

looking back to this section of coast around Gribun, which again portrays the drama of this volcano-created landscape.

40 A brief interlude back in Salen to enjoy this northwards panorama which, among other things, includes the retired, decaying boats on the left. Aros Castle, a stone 13th-century hall house and

courtyard fortress built by the MacDonalds, can be made out in the centre distance. It's low tide on the Sound of Mull and in the distance the hills of Ardnamurchan are visible.

42 Returning to our circuit of western Mull, the rocky outcrops across the water are on the little island of Inch Kenneth, named after the saint who built a monastery there in the 6th century.

From further on and further up, the higher end of Inch Kenneth and the house built in the 1930s **43** by Sir Harold Boulton, writer of the Skye Boat Song. Later on it was the home of Unity Mitford.

44 Continuing south via an inland pass brings us to the north side of Loch Scridain, another of Mull's great sea lochs. This is the relatively pastoral landscape around Tiroran House.

Tiroran is the starting point of the increasingly adventurous walk to the Burg scenic coastline.
This particularly pretty waterfall is passed at about the half-way mark.

46 Part of the adventure is the prospect of seeing some of Mull's feral goats that roam this shoreline. They blend with the rocks quite well, but those impressive horns are hard to miss!

Basalt and the curiously geometric shapes it formed when cooling are a recurring theme of **47**
Mull's geology. One such feature is this basalt 'wheel' that can be seen on the Burg coastline.

48 It's easier to get a sense of the fierce terrain that has to be conquered from the other side of the loch: final destination is to the left of where the left-hand waterfall hits the shore.

And the reason for all this effort? The 12m/40ft tall Fossil Tree is where molten basalt has acquired **49** the impression of the tree over which it flowed – a geological wonder!

50 Now to eastern Mull: between Craignure and Lochdon stands Torosay Castle, completed in 1858 by the eminent architect David Bryce in the Scottish Baronial style. The castle is not open to the public.

Towering over eastern Mull, at 766m/2513ft Dun da Ghaoithe is the island's third-highest peak. **51**
Seen here from the south, it is embellished by the clouds it has helped to create.

52 Duart Castle stands proudly on a cliff top guarding the Sound of Mull, enjoying one of the most spectacular positions on the west coast of Scotland. This shot was taken from the Mull ferry.

Duart Castle has been the base of the Clan Maclean's sea-borne power for over 400 years. **53**
It is one of a chain of castles that runs up the Sound of Mull to Mingary Castle in Ardnamurchan.

54 Duart Castle's fine Banqueting Hall. The castle lay abandoned for at least 150 years until purchased by Sir Fitzroy Maclean in 1910. He then set about the enormous task of restoring the building,

a process that continues to this day. Major repairs were undertaken from 1991 to 1995, but work on the castle goes on. Pictured here is the State Bedroom.

56 This is the very pleasing view from the grounds of Duart Castle across Duart Bay towards Mull's eastern mountains, with Dun da Ghaoithe again visible in the distance.

58 Mull does not get a great deal of snow, but here we see Ben More with a goodly coating.

Mull has a large deer population. In this dawn view near Lochdon, **59** a few of them enjoy the peace of the sea shore.

60 As we begin to track across the south of the island, a visit to Lochbuie reveals a variety of points of interest, including Mull's only stone circle. It dates from the late Neolithic or early Bronze Age.

The small settlement of Lochbuie looks out over this idyllic scene. **61**
It takes its name from Loch Buie, a sheltered south-facing sea loch.

62 St Kilda's church was built by MacLaine of Lochbuie in 1876. Its interior contains much of interest and its peaceful ambience embraces those who enter.

There are two beaches at Lochbuie, the southerly one being known as Laggan Sands, **63** seemingly more often enjoyed by the local cattle than humans.

64 Lochbuie House, built in 1793, is overlooked by Ben Buie. Inset: several types of orchid grow on Mull, this being the Heath Spotted variety.

The next excursion is to Carsaig, further along Mull's southern coast where, on the right day, the bay **65** can take on a distinctly Mediterranean look. But the main reason for coming here

66 is to visit the hugely impressive sea-cut rock arches four miles further along the coast. Pictured here is the first one, long and cavernous at around 6m/20ft high. Beyond this arch, the second one cuts

a more shapely and sculpted appearance. Once again, basalt columns feature large in this landscape. **67**
Just how much longer will the prominent 'chimney' survive?

68 The walk to Carsaig Arches is likely to be enhanced by sightings of the local wildlife. Left: a shag poses politely. Right: an otter just gets on with its fish supper.

The journey westwards continues along the southern shore of Loch Scridain, surrounded by autumn **69** hues and with Ben More drawing the eye to its shapely heights.

70 We are now in the district known as the Ross of Mull, where the village of Bunessan wraps around the head of Loch na Làthaich. Bunessan was established as a fishing station in the late 1700s.

From Bunessan, it's worth taking a small detour south to see Ardalanish Bay. For those who like **71**
their beaches a little more rocky, this one certainly fits the bill – great colours too.

72 And finally, the long and winding road through Mull reaches the island's most westerly point at the village of Fionnphort. As well as the arresting foreground, the scene that unfolds gives a first sight

of Iona, final destination for so many of the travellers who have ventured this far. The ferry waits to carry them over the Sound of Iona.

74 The Iona ferry is nearing Fionnphort pier on a bright day of somewhat lively seas. The smaller boat behind is one of those that sails to Staffa and other local islands.

Few places generate such a sense of 'arrival' as Iona. From the ferry and across a welcome-mat of stunningly coloured water, the village of Baile Mor waits to greet us.

76 How do you describe Iona? – magical, enchanting, sacred, peaceful, a very special place? When treated to scenes like this minutes after stepping off the ferry, here's the answer!

Iona's chief claim to fame is as a site of Christian pilgrimage. Here are the remains of the Nunnery founded by Reginald MacDonald of Islay around 1200.

78 Left: Maclean's Cross, erected c.1500, is a wayside prayer-cross situated beyond the Nunnery.
Right: the present-day liking for less permanent structures, as seen at the Bay at the Back of the Ocean.

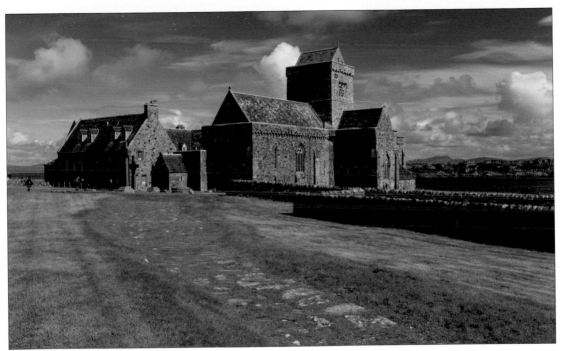

For the pilgrim, this is journey's end: Iona Abbey, founded by St Columba in 563AD, a place of **79** prayer and worship for people from all over the world. It has been through long years of ruin

80 but restoration of the Abbey Church began in 1902, with work on the nave being completed by 1910. Here is the candlelit Abbey interior, specially decorated for the Harvest Service.

There are five stained-glass windows in the abbey, one of which is back on p.7. The other four **81** depict, from left to right, St Columba, St Patrick, St Brigid and St Margaret.

82 Dawn over Iona Abbey. The Iona Community was founded in Glasgow and Iona in 1938 by the Revd George MacLeod, minister, visionary and prophetic witness for peace.

Inside view of Iona Abbey Cloister. The facing page shows the garth, the grassed area within the
cloister, on which stands a bronze sculpture by Lithuanian sculptor Jacob Lipchitz which bears

84 the inscription 'Jacob Lipchitz, Jew, faithful to the religion of his ancestors, has made this Virgin for the better understanding of human beings so that the Spirit may prevail'.

Top left: column-top detail, cloister; top right: tomb of the 8th Duke of Argyll who initiated the abbey's restoration; lower left: stone bearing earliest known Christian sign; lower right: the abbey's 'quiet corner'.

86 Iona is a small island approximately 3½ miles long and no more than 1½ miles wide. The highest point is the 100m/328ft Dun I, from where this view takes in the north end of the island.

One of Iona's more enigmatic and therefore much searched-for spots is the Well of Eternal Youth, **87** to the north-east of Dun I's summit. (Not easy to find – take advice from the locals!)

88 Look south from Dun I and this splendid panorama is revealed. The abbey is picked out in the evening light; the ferry departs on its last crossing of the day; the Sound of Iona leads the eye to

a dark horizon and Fionnphort can just be seen on the far side. The peace of this tranquil place deepens as the day draws to a close.

90 Columba reputedly landed at this bay at the southern tip of Iona, which consequently now bears his name. Modern-day visitors have arranged stone settings intended to symbolize what Iona means to them.

Left: and so to the final adventure of this tour, a trip on the MV Iolaire to Staffa. **91**
Right: soon after setting sail, a pod of dolphins appears and swims alongside for a while.

92 The tiny island of Staffa, famous for its columnar basalt formations and Fingal's Cave, seen towards the right. This was the inspiration for Felix Mendelssohn's Hebrides Overture.

Left: looking into the depths of Fingal's Cave. Right: the view from inside looking out. **93**
Great care is required here – falling into the sea is fraught with dangers, one of which is . . .

94 . . . the way the sea builds up into this huge wave as it is funnelled through the narrowing channel near the mouth of the cave. On the other side, a basalt outcrop shows off its precise shapes.

Left: a visit to Staffa allows time for an exploration of its plateau, from where the various cave entrances can be seen. Right: adventure over, it's time, a little wistfully, to rejoin the boat. **95**

Published 2015 by Ness Publishing, 47 Academy Street, Elgin, Moray, IV30 1LR
Phone 01343 549663 www.nesspublishing.co.uk

All photographs © Colin and Eithne Nutt except pp.30 (both) & 68 (right) © Andrew Oldacre;
p.19 © Belinda Hale; p.58 © Steve Kirk; p.59 © Diana Oldacre

Text © Colin Nutt
ISBN 978-1-906549-28-2

Front cover: Iona from Fionnphort; p.1: part of Eas Fors waterfall; p.4: sheep at Aros; this page: Bishop's House in Baile Mor, Iona; back cover: view from Fionnphort towards the island of Bac Mor, known locally as the Dutchman's Cap

For a list of websites and phone numbers please turn over > > > >

Websites and phone numbers (where available) of featured places in alphabetical order:

Bishop's House, Iona: www.island-retreats.org/iona (T) 01681 700111
Calgary Art in Nature: www.calgary.co.uk/art (T) 01668 400256
Duart Castle: www.duartcastle.com (T) 01680 812309
Dun Ara Castle: canmore.rcahms.gov.uk/en/site/22069/details/mull+dun+ara/
Fossil Tree: www.isle-of-mull.net
Glengorm Castle: www.glengormcastle.co.uk (T) 01688 302321
Iona: www.ionahistory.org.uk
Iona Abbey and Nunnery: www.historic-scotland.gov.uk (T) 01681 700512
Iona Community: iona.org.uk (T) 01681 700404
Isle of Mull: www.isle-of-mull.net; www.mullmagic.com
Isle of Ulva: www.isleofulva.com (T) 01688 500264
Lochbuie: www.lochbuie.com
Macquarie's Mausoleum: www.isle-of-mull.net
Old Byre Heritage Centre: www.old-byre.co.uk (T) 01688 400229
Staffa: www.staffatours.com; www.staffatrips.co.uk (T) 01681 700358
Tobermory: www.tobermory.co.uk
Tobermory Distillery: tobermorydistillery.com
Torosay Castle: www.isle-of-mull.net
Ulva Boathouse: www.theboathouseulva.co.uk (T) 01688 500241

Further places and organisations of interest re. Mull and Iona:
Sea-Life cruises: whalewatchwithus.com
www.undiscoveredscotland.co.uk
www.walkhighlands.co.uk
Wildlife boat trips: www.mullcharters.com (01680 300444)